Revelation

Worship the Lamb

Sarah K. Howley

Flaming Dove Press

Flaming Dove Press
an imprint of
InspiritEncourage LLC
1520 Belle View Blvd #5081
Alexandria, VA 22307
www.inspiritencourage.com

ISBN 978-1-960793-36-2 (e-pub)
ISBN 978-1-960793-37-9 (paperback)
ISBN 978-1-960793-38-6 (large print)

Printed in the United States of America

Library of Congress Control Number: 2025916569

Contents

Welcome

to this Study of Revelation

The apostle John likely wrote this book around A.D. 90 to strengthen the faith of believers who were facing persecution and beginning to compromise on their faith. Having experienced divinely inspired visions, he recorded them and shared them with the seven churches in Asia Minor offering them hope through the revelation of Christ's kingship and eventual return to redeem His people and judge evil. The book also includes intense imagery and prophecies about the end times. Since it includes letters, symbolic imagery as well as prophecy, Revelation is generally classified as apocalyptic literature but is included in this collection of studies that see the links between letters and the Old Testament.

Though many view Revelation primarily as a book about the end times, it was ultimately written to reveal Jesus Christ and his glory. Revelation means 'unveiling', and John's intention was to deepen believers' understanding of who Jesus was, is, and is to come.

Not all scholars agree on how to read Revelation, and it has become a controversial book. The intent of this study is to view the forest rather than the trees, developing a big picture rather than agreeing on a single interpretation. This study encourages using Scripture to interpret Scripture, rather than relying on a single framework for interpretation.

Across its 404 verses, Revelation contains at least 500 allusions and references to the Old Testament. Because of the sheer number, this study focuses on only a selection of those. Reading Revelation without familiarity with the Old Testament can feel like jumping into the final installment of a trilogy—without the first two, many themes and references are easily missed. The chosen passages are intended to highlight John's message and deepen our awareness of Revelation's connections to earlier biblical writings, all while keeping the broader picture in view.

Each session opens with warm-up introductory questions, has a reading from Revelation and questions related to the passage. Then the study highlights the linked Old Testament passages and some reflection questions. Each study session ends with considerations for personal application. Additional tips and suggestions on approaching the study for individuals and groups follow.

Suggestions for this Study

This study is designed for individual or small group study and is composed of 15 sessions. It is designed to encourage thought and discussion of the scripture, encouraging individuals and groups seeking God to have conversations about the text. For 'You will seek me and find me when you seek me with all your heart,' as Jeremiah 29:13 says.

General Guidelines for Individual Study

1. Open each session with prayer. Ask God to speak through his Word.

2. Respond to the introductory questions that focus on the theme of the session and what God says in the main reading.

3. Read the passage more than once, perhaps in different translations. Using different translations can offer expanded viewpoints on the meaning of the original text. This study uses the New International Version (NIV) as the basis of questions

and quotes. However, any version may be used to provide insight and assist in revealing meaning.

4. This study is designed to offer a starting point for discovery of what God has to say to you through his Word. Because the study looks at how the Old Testament is reflected in the epistles, there are observation and interpretation questions about the readings in Revelation and then about the links in the Old Testament, as well as comparisons between the passages. These are followed by application questions for personal reflection and group discussion. Writing your responses will provide clarity and focus your thoughts on the verses.

5. Use a Bible dictionary or other reference books to look up any unfamiliar words, places, or names.

General Guidelines for Group Study

1. Come to sessions prepared. Some groups will choose to read and respond ahead of time then gather and discuss together; others will gather to read and discuss together. Before beginning, agree how you would like to proceed so all are prepared.

2. Be an active participant in the group by sharing your thoughts and responses to the questions. Groups often have members who are in different places in their walk with Christ and each perspective should be valued.

3. Listen to each other. Consider the amount of time that is available for all to share and be careful not to dominate the conversation.

4. Be open-minded. Participants are encouraged to be open to learning and sharing, even expecting alternate viewpoints. The Bible serves as the foundation of this study and hearing other perspectives may challenge your own understanding. When differing views arise, the focus should remain on listening to each other and encouraging one another to wrestle with difficult passages and concepts rather than building consensus. Full agreement about everything in Revelation may be challenging given that it offers numerous images that theologians have argued over for centuries without coming to agreement.

5. Maintain group confidentiality. For participants to be willing to share and grow, the trust level in the group must be high. Do not share what is shared in the group outside of the group unless permission is given to do so.

6. Expect God to meet you in the study. His Word is living and active (Heb. 4:12) and he is present when we gather in his name (Matt. 18:20).

Introduction

People have many different understandings of Revelation. What are your own expectations as you begin this study? What do you already feel, think or believe about this book?

Much of Revelation uses symbolic imagery and prophecy, often without clear explanation. On a scale of 1 (very comfortable with mystery) to 10 (very uncomfortable), how do you feel about that kind of uncertainty?

Session 1: A Revelation of Christ

Revelation 1:1-20

Opening

Imagine Christ in the throne room of heaven, what do you think that room would look like? How would you describe the physical form of Jesus in that throne room?

When people face crisis or uncertainty, what kinds of messages (perhaps social media posts or texts to friends and family) do they tend to write or share? What is the typical focus of those messages?

John wrote this letter to seven churches in Asia Minor, or modern-day Turkey while he was in exile for preaching the gospel. From this place of isolation, he wrote these words as blessings and encouragement to believers facing hardship. The vision he recorded began with Jesus himself, described in vivid, awe-inspiring imagery. This is the first of many images in Revelation that stir wonder and worship.

Read Revelation 1:1-20.

Reading Questions

What (or who) does this book reveal? Who was the revelation intended for and why?

Revelation 1:4-6 is called a doxology, or "praise", to the Trinity. Identify the phrases that reference and acclaim the Father, the Son, and the Holy Spirit.

How did John describe himself in Revelation 1:9? What does it tell us about the readers?

What is most striking about the figure that John described in Revelation 1:12-15?

How did the person that John saw then describe themselves?

How does Revelation 1:19 outline the book's contents?

According to this passage, what do the seven stars and seven lampstands represent?

Old Testament Links

The opening line of Revelation states that Jesus was revealed in this book. From the greeting, John described images and used symbols that draw on other biblical references to Jesus. However, the use of imagery and symbols sometimes makes it more challenging to identify him. As you consider the following passages and questions, remember that the book was intended to focus attention on the person and glory of Jesus Christ.

Read Daniel 7:13-14 and Zechariah 12:10-14, which reflect Revelation 1:7. How do these verses demonstrate Jesus' elevated status and glorify him?

Read Daniel 7:9, 10:6 and Ezekiel 1:24-27 How do these verses unveil the splendor and majesty of Christ found in Revelation 1:13-16?

Application

The imagery in Revelation 1:12-13 placed Jesus among the seven churches along with seven angels for the churches. What picture does this give of his involvement in the church today?

What encouragement can be taken from Jesus "alive for ever and ever" and holding the keys of death?

Session 2: Renew Your First Love

Revelation 2:1-29

Opening

What are three things you might expect Christ to compliment the church on if he wrote a letter to us today?

How would you imagine Christ would introduce himself in such a letter?

This chapter and the next include letters dictated by Jesus to seven churches in what is now modern-day Turkey. Each message offers both correction and encouragement, along with a promise for those who remain faithful. Together, they show

Jesus' unwavering care for his people and call believers to respond with steady, enduring faith.

Read Revelation 2:1-29.

Reading Questions

In this passage, Jesus dictated four letters to churches in Asia Minor. For each one, note the way Jesus introduced himself, what he commended the church for doing, what warning he gave regarding negative or bad things present in the church, and how he encouraged the particular church.

The Church in Ephesus

Jesus' Introduction:

Commendation:

Warning:

Encouragement:

The Church in Smyrna

Jesus' Introduction:

Commendation:

Warning:

Encouragement:

The Church in Pergamum

Jesus' Introduction:

Commendation:

Warning:

Encouragement:

The Church in Thyatira

Jesus' Introduction:

Commendation:

Warning:

Encouragement:

Old Testament Links

Who Jesus is was a theme of this letter. To each of the churches, he presented himself in slightly different ways yet interacted with them in a familiar way. Though prophetic and history books do not generally contain prescriptions for us, they may present patterns of God's behavior and interactions with man that we can observe.

If Daniel 1:12-14 is considered a pattern of what happens in testing, how might that pattern encourage the Smyrnean believers who suffered "ten days" (Revelation 2:10)?

Revelation 1:12 referred to "him who has the sharp, double-edged sword." What characteristic(s) did this refer to according to Psalm 149:6-9?

Application

Jesus' warnings were given to encourage the churches' faithfulness. What areas of your life most challenge your faithfulness to him?

These short letters to the churches focused often on enduring and repenting. How have these themes shown up in your life recently?

Session 3: Come Alive

Revelation 3:1-22

Opening

What are three things you might expect Christ to rebuke the church about if he wrote a letter to us today?

How would you describe a "life-filled" church? How would you describe a "dead" church?

Jesus' letters to the churches continue in this session. The letters reemphasize the themes of faithfulness and repentance, as well as depending on the Lord for strength and perseverance. These same lessons speak to believers today, reminding us to rely on him to remain strong in faith.

Read Revelation 3:1-22.

Reading Questions

In this passage, Jesus dictated three additional letters to churches in Asia Minor. For each one, note the way Jesus introduced himself, what he commended the church for doing, what warning he gave regarding negative or bad things present in the church, and how he encouraged the particular church.

The Church in Sardis

Jesus' Introduction:

Commendation:

Warning:

Encouragement:

The Church in Philadelphia

Jesus' Introduction:

Commendation:

Warning:

Encouragement:

The Church in Laodicea

Jesus' Introduction:

Commendation:

Warning:

Encouragement:

Old Testament Links

You may have sung how Jesus is "all in all," which is a great profession of worship. The repetition of Jesus introducing himself offered the reader the opportunity to see the various "alls" that Jesus is. These introductions enlarge his role or authority in each church letter.

Isaiah 22:15-25 describes the use of the key of David, as referenced in Revelation 3:7. What does this short passage indicate about the role of Jesus as keyholder?

Read Proverbs 3:11-12 and compare these verses to Revelation 3:19. How does the emphasis on relationship soften the rebuke and discipline?

Application

The church in Sardis had things left unfinished (Revelation 3:2). Consider what things are in-progress (actively working) and which may have been left "unfinished" (abandoned) in your life. How can you revive the work in these parts of life?

As noted, Jesus commended each of the churches in his letters. Imagine he wrote a letter to commend you for what you're doing well. How would He commend you (1) in what you have done well and (2) in ways you are becoming more Christlike?

Session 4: A Glimpse of the Throne

Revelation 4:1–5:14

Opening

How is the worth of something determined? Is it any different when determining the worth of a person?

What imagery is often associated with depictions of heaven?

John's account of his testimony of what he saw is full of rich depictions, even if they aren't easy to for our minds to visualize. In the readings for today, it's as if we were taken to heaven with

John and provided a glimpse of what he saw. The descriptions are not enough to fully understand our future but offer us the purpose of our heavenly calling: worshipping God.

Read Revelation 4:1–5:14.

Reading Questions

John used lots of descriptions in chapter 4 but now look for the basic things or people that he sees. List those that he sees "in the Spirit."

What were these beings doing in his vision in Revelation Chapter 4?

What did John say about the purpose of creation in Revelation 4:11?

Why was John weeping unconsolably in Revelation 5:4?

Describe the image of the lamb John presented. What reason was given for the lamb's worthiness?

What did the passage say was the incense the creatures and elders held?

What were the creatures doing again at the end of Revelation chapter 5?

Old Testament Links

Revelation Chapters 4 and 5 tie together various imagery used to highlight the perfect and worthy nature of Jesus to open the scroll. Taken together, the images in their context help us to understand the character of God and why he is worthy of all praise. Throughout the Old Testament, the image of the lamb points to Jesus as the perfect sacrifice, faithful and true to God's covenant.

Read Genesis 9:11-17 and Ezekiel 1:28. (If you would like a refresher on Noah and the flood, feel free to read Genesis Chapters 6-8 as well.) What did the rainbow represent according to the passages? What should the depiction of a rainbow in today's passage bring to the minds of original readers of Revelation?

Read Genesis 22:6-14; Exodus 12:5-7, 12-13; Isaiah 53:5-7 and note the characteristics of the lamb. How do those characteristics make the lamb worthy to open the scroll?

Application

Awe and surrender characterize the praise demonstrated in the throne room. What keeps you from worshipping in awe and surrender like the elders?

What aspect of Jesus most moves you to praise? How can you express that this week?

Session 5: Six Seals Opened

Revelation 6:1-17

Opening

In ancient times, wax seals were placed on important documents to verify their authenticity. What methods are used today to mark the authenticity of important documents?

Justice is a complex idea. Some see justice as consequences for wrongdoing. Others believe it must include a change of heart or even restoration to those who were harmed. In old westerns, justice was often portrayed as retribution. What do you think justice means? How do you think it is best carried out?

This chapter begins the part of Revelation referred to as The Tribulation. While it does speak of fearful and terrible judgement, this is the beginning of God making things right. This is done by ending what is wrong on the earth, so that God can establish what is good and right. This is not about fearfulness, but about justice and hope.

Read Revelation 6:1-17.

Reading Questions

As you read of the first four seals and the horsemen that are sent out, note the horse color, what the horseman's name or representation was and what he carried and did on the earth.

First Seal

Horse Color

Name or Representation

Action

Second Seal

    Horse Color

    Name or Representation

    Action

Third Seal

    Horse Color

    Name or Representation

    Action

Fourth Seal

    Horse Color

    Name or Representation

    Action

When the fifth seal was opened, what happened? What was their cry?

What was the effect of the sixth seal on the earth and sky? How did the people of earth respond?

Old Testament Links

When tribulation was spoken of in the times of the Old Testament, it was usually accompanied with exhortations to return to God's way. These were not merely punishments but expressions of godly discipline – just and purposeful, rooted in covenantal relationship. God's justice was not detached from his desire to restore his people; it was a reminder that judgement is part of redemption.

In Daniel 9:24, Joel 2:10-14, and Zephaniah 1:14-2:3, God revealed his plans for the future and desires for his people. Note the purposes and desires and how they connect to Revelation 6.

In Zechariah 1:8-17 is a prophet's vision of four horsemen. What conditions did they find in the earth and how did the angel respond to their report? What message was the prophet told to share?

Application

The martyrs who were shown following the opening of the fifth seal cry out for justice. They had been waiting for God's action. What does it mean to trust that God will make things right, even if it isn't yet seen?

The glimmers of hope in this chapter of Revelation seem most visible when we recognize the call to return to God seen in John's use of Old Testament allusions. What might "returning to God" look like in your lives today?

Session 6: Salvation Belongs to our God

Revelation 7:1-8:1

Opening

What do you do to mark that something important belongs to you? How do you protect important things or people?

How do you define worship in Christian context? What is it and how is it carried out?

This chapter offers a glimpse of the hope that rises in the midst of tribulation. What was hinted at before—the protection and salvation of God's people—begins to unfold more clearly. Those who are sealed and those who come through the tribulation are seen serving God. The image of a great multitude in white robes suggests a hope that spans far beyond one group or moment.

Read Revelation 7:1-17-8:1.

Reading Questions

What were the four angels told to do?

What group of people received the seal of God?

What was the multitude doing in the throne room?

Who were those in white robes, according to Revelation 7:14?

What promises were the people in white robes given?

What happened following the opening of the seventh seal?

Old Testament Links

From Genesis to Revelation, the Bible tells a unified story of God's faithful love and His desire to dwell with and care for His people. The vision in Revelation 7 draws on powerful Old Testament imagery—scenes where God sets apart His people, responds to suffering, and reaffirms His promises. These echoes remind us that Revelation isn't a break from what came before but a continuation of God's long-standing relationship with His people—a relationship rooted in both justice and mercy.

Ezekiel 9:3-6 presents a similar picture to that of the opening scene of Revelation 7. What was the apparent purpose of the seals?

God made promises similar to those in Revelation 7:16-17 in the Old Testament. How do these promises differ from those in Isaiah 25:4-9, 40:11, 49:10?

Application

In Revelation 7:15-17, the people from the tribulation were promised freedom from hardships of hunger, thirst, and heat. What promises of God are comforting to you?

The multitude in white robes in Revelation 7 came through great tribulation. We face trials and tribulations even now; what helps you remain faithful when life is difficult or uncertain?

Session 7: Six Trumpets Sound

Revelation 8:2-9:21

Opening

What is the definition of repent? How is it different from regret?

Proverbs 25:2 says, "It is the glory of God to conceal a matter; to search out a matter is the glory of kings." What is the reason for searching out understanding, according to this verse? How might this help explain the difficulty of understanding passages from Revelation?

The trumpets in today's passage shake the earth, sounding warnings through escalating destruction. John's vision doesn't point to mindless ruin, but to something more purposeful. Even in the midst of what is unclear and unsettling, hope is not absent.

Read Revelation 8:2-9:21,

Reading Questions

What does Revelation 8:3-5 illustrate about the power of prayer?

Summarize the result of each trumpet blast:

First trumpet

Second trumpet

Third trumpet

Fourth trumpet

Fifth trumpet. Who was spared?

Sixth trumpet

God's purpose for these trumpet judgements was given in
Revelation 9:20-21. What was the intent?

Old Testament Links

The trumpet judgments in Revelation echo scenes that would
have been familiar from earlier Scripture—waters turned to
blood, skies darkened, locusts swarming. These signs are not
new; they trace back to Old Testament passages of devastation.
What was history or prophecy now reappears on a greater scale
and with renewed intensity.

How did the trumpet judgments reflect the plagues of Egypt Exodus 7:20-23, 9:22-24?

Joel 1:2-7, 2:1-5, 3:12-13 describes an invading army and compares it to locusts. Note the similarities in the passages. In what way do the passages from Joel and Revelation call for a response?

Application

Have there been times in your life when unplanned events or challenging times made you more aware of your need to return to God? What did repentance look like in that season—for your heart, your choices, or your relationships?

When the world feels overwhelming or chaotic, what helps you stay spiritually grounded? Are there practices or truths that help you hold to hope rather than fear?

Session 8: The Final Trumpet

Revelation 10:1-11:19

Opening

Describe how secrets can be both good and bad.

Deuteronomy 29:29 says some things belong to God alone. What does the verse say about the purpose of revealed scripture? How do you feel about the idea that God chose to keep some things hidden? How can we stay grounded when people claim to have "new revelations" or "secrets" from Scripture?

Today's passage presents an interlude before the final trumpet sounds at the end of Chapter 11. John was told to keep this part of the vision quiet yet is also told that a mystery will be accomplished. In the midst of this odd mix of secrecy, two witness are sent to throughout the earth revealing God through their testimony. The hope that again rises from the witnesses who are sent to the unsaved reminds us of the goodness of God.

Read Revelation 10:1-11:19.

Reading Questions

What does the description of the angel and his stance say of his position in heaven?

What had been delayed but would be revealed or seen soon?.

As John ate the scroll, it tasted of honey yet turned sour in his stomach. What might the symbolism of the tase say of understanding or "digesting" prophesy?

What powers did the witness have?

What would happen to the witnesses when they finished their testimony?

What was the result of the seventh trumpet?

Old Testament Links

The striking images found in this passage call to mind the prophets of old – also told to eat a scroll, to speak boldly, and to forge onward even when the word was rejected. God's consistent pattern of sending messengers to reach the resistant world reflects his love for all and his desire to be known. In the darkness of tribulation, the obedience of the witnesses shines as the beacon of hope.

Read Ezekiel 2:3–3:3. How does Ezekiel's commission help you understand the role of the witnesses and the resistance they experienced?

Jonah was a messenger sent to a wicked and harsh place to testify. Read Jonah 3:1-10. How does this story guide our understanding of what God hopes to do when he sends witnesses?

Application

The consistent sending of witnesses to speak of God and his goodness throughout the Bible encourages us to speak faithfully. Where might God be inviting you to speak of him?

John was told to keep hidden part of his vision. How do you respond when the future seems hidden or God's plans unknown? What helps you trust him in dark times?

Session 9: Dragon's Defeat

Revelation 12:1-13:18

Opening

A testimony recounts personal experience. Have you seen someone give a testimony in court or have you given a testimony about a product or restaurant on social media? In some ways even a product review on a website is a testimony. Tell about an experience giving your testimony. Why did you feel you needed to do this?

Have you ever seen something that looked real but turned out to be a fake? What kinds of things make imitations convincing at first glance?

John's vision is just that – a vision, not a film reel of what did happen or will happen. It is full of symbols and signs that suggest things but are left open for interpretation. Revelation 12 and 13 are full of such imagery. Theologians for centuries have offered ideas of what these symbols represent, but few have come to solid agreement. Outlining what is seen and described will help clarify the vision rather than trying to interpret them.

Read Revelation 12:1-13:18.

Reading Questions

Two signs are depicted in Revelation 12:1-6 and 12:13-13:1. Describe the symbols and what happened to each?

Who defeated the dragon and his army?

How were they overcome, according to Revelation 12:11?

Testimony is mentioned twice in Revelation 12. What is the result of testimony according to these verses?

Two beasts were described in John's vision in Revelation 13. Who gave them their authority?

How did earth's inhabitants respond to the beasts?

Old Testament Links

The symbolism of the dragon and beasts may not be fully clear, but their power and influence over people are unmistakable in John's vision. These would not have been unfamiliar images to those reading the Revelation of Jesus Christ. Deception and misused authority had already appeared in both visions and the history of God's people - and John was shown more would come.

Read Daniel 7:1-8, 19-27 and compare what's in the text with the beast of Revelation 13:2-8. What similarities are there in the visions?

Both visions describe a time where power opposing God is allowed to rise for a specified time. What do you notice about the people of God during that time and when that oppression ends?

Application

Testimony plays an important role in the victory over oppression and the powers of evil. Take a moment to write down a simple testimony of God's presence or help in your life. You might reflect on a time of stress, trial, or uncertainty, and how God met you in that moment. Keep it brief as just a few sentences is enough to hold something true and shareable.

Now, write down the names of two people you can begin to pray for—people who may need to hear the hope in your testimony. Ask God to open a door for conversation and prepare their hearts as well as your own.

Session 10: Sing a New Song

Revelation 14:1-20

Opening

Music is a special form of communication that often carries emotion or meaning. Certain songs may come to mind that mark particular celebrations, sorrows or hopes. Can you think of a moment (in film, real life, or history) where music shaped how the event was understood or remembered?

Farmers spend many days working to prepare the soil and plant a crop, tending to it all along. But harvest comes only when a crop is ripe, after waiting for fullness of time. When harvesting occurs it's often accompanied by celebration. What are some ways cultures or communities celebrate harvest?

John's vision continues with the appearance of the lamb and his followers – likely those from Chapter 7. Revelation 14 is filled with messages for the earth and the faithful, delivered by angels of God. The final image is striking: a winepress of wrath poured out with great finality, yet this harvest comes only when ripe.

Read Revelation 14:1-20.

Reading Questions

List three things the 144,000 did in Revelation 14:1-5.

In Revelation 14:6-13, three angels delivered God's messages. Summarize each of those.

First Message

Second Message

Third Message

What promise is made to God's people?

What crop did each heavenly being gather?

Old Testament Links

Three angels offer opportunities for repentance before the winepress of judgement comes to the earth. Yet these were not the first proclamations of good news or calls to return to God – they echo messages spoken long ago in the Old Testament. The invitation still sounds for the earth to hear: the kingdom of God is at hand.

Read Joel 3:12-14. These verses mention the "valley of decision." What decision have the people made? What decision have the reapers made? How does this expand your understanding of the harvest in Revelation 14?

Isaiah 55:6–11 could be considered a "gospel passage" in the Old Testament. Consider what parts of the passage reflect good news, and how they serve as an early example of God's word going out long before the harvest was ripe.

Application

Revelation 14:12 says that "patient endurance" is necessary. Where do you need God to help you endure in your life right now? What keeps your eye on Jesus to endure in hard times?

What kind of music playlist would you build around key events in your life? What emotion or feelings would you assign to the various events?

Session 11: Seven Bowls of Judgement

Revelation 15:1-16:21

Opening

Some endings carry a sense of weight—like finishing university, completing a big project, or reaching the final moment of a long journey. Can you think of a time when something came to a close in a way that felt especially significant? What made that moment stand out from all the steps that led up to it?

How do people respond to significant global or natural events? What kinds of emotions or behaviors often surface? Which of those emotions end up on social media and which are held tightly?

In Revelation we see that God's judgment has unfolded in stages—first through the seven seals, then the seven trumpets, and now through seven bowls of wrath. The earlier visions revealed chaos, rebellion, and warning. Now, with the bowls, judgment is poured out in full. The witnesses have spoken, and the gospel has gone out; the judgement is described as just and true.

Read Revelation 15:1-16:21.

Reading Questions

A group stood near a sea of glass mixed with fire. Who were they and what were they doing?

What happened at the temple before the wrath was poured out?

How did the angels and the altar describe God's judgements?

Where was each bowl of wrath poured and what was its result?

First Bowl

Second Bowl

Third Bowl

Fourth Bowl

Fifth Bowl

Sixth Bowl

Seventh Bowl

How did people respond to the final plagues?

Who gathered the kings of the east? Where did they gather?

Old Testament Links

Long periods of mercy followed by judgement often appear
in the Old Testament. From the Israelites in the wilderness to
words of the prophets, God continually called on his people
to turn from their ways and return to him. These repeated
invitations reveal something of God's character – he is patient,
persistent, just, and always desiring restoration. The vision in
today's passage echoes that pattern - where God's character was
evident.

Read Ezekiel 18:20-32. What do you notice about how God's justice is described in this passage? How does it help understand the judgement poured out in Revelation 15-16?

Read Proverbs 19:3 and 24:10-12. What do these verses say about human actions and responsibility? How do they also reflect God's awareness of our hearts and his judgement?

Application

In the Bible, the number seven often represents completion. In this case, seven bowls of wrath represented the fulfillment of God's judgement. What emotion does it evoke to reflect on the vision of God carrying out his promise of justice for the wrongs done to you?

God's justice doesn't always come when we want it, but it does come. What helps you trust his timing when justice or resolution seems slow in coming?

Session 12: The Downfall of Babylon

Revelation 17:1-18:24

Opening

What kinds of things make someone seem like a faithful or loyal friend? Are there habits or characteristics that build that kind of relationship?

Some places, brands, or experiences seem to be more glamourous or commanding. What makes something feel powerful or appealing to a wide group of people?

The images presented in these two chapters tell the story of a powerful woman, a war, and her downfall. The devotion she received, the strength she displayed, and eventually the betrayal by those supporting her make for a complex account of the vision. However, the framework of the story reminds us of the ultimate victor and what truly endures.

Read Revelation 17:1–18:24.

Reading Questions

What was the name and profession of the woman in the first verses of Revelation 17? What was she drinking?

What did the angel say was necessary for John in this vision (Revelation 17:9)?

What information was given about the beast (Revelation 17:9-13)?

What hope does Revelation 17:14 offer?

What happened to Babylon at the end of Revelation 17?

Three groups of people lament the end of Lady Babylon. Name them and how they profited from her.

Who cheered the end of Babylon?

How would you categorize that which "will never again" in Babylon, Revelation 18:21-23?

Old Testament Links

The woman in Revelation 17 was called a prostitute, an image that is found in several Old Testament passages. The Scripture uses the language of prostitution in striking ways, often connected to warnings from the prophets. As you read more about Babylon, it offers insight into what John saw in his vision.

Read Isaiah 1:21-23 and Jeremiah 3:6-10, 14-18. What actions qualified the group to be named a prostitute? How does the image of Jerusalem contrast to that of Babylon in Revelation 17-18?

Read Isaiah 14:1-8. What similarities are there between this passage and Revelation 17-18? How is the Revelation imagery expanded in this Old Testament passage?

Application

In what areas of life do you find it most difficult to stay faithful to your values or commitments, especially when those around you may not share them? What helps hold you steady in those values?

When something seems powerful, successful, or impressive, what helps you discern whether it is also aligned with God's character? What does it look like to follow Jesus in a world that often rewards status, visibility, or control?

Session 13: Triumphant Return

Revelation 19:1-16

Opening

Think about a time when a crowd erupted in celebration—like at a championship win, a graduation ceremony, or even a standing ovation after a powerful performance. What does public praise or acclaim look like? How do crowds react to things done well?

Weddings demonstrate unity, joy and covenant. What meaningful or memorable traditions have you seen at weddings?

The crowds roared. The elders joined in the praise and worship. Together, they celebrated the wedding feast of the Lamb. This portion of Revelation is filled with triumph and awe for our God who is worthy of all glory and praise. Jesus appeared with names of power and the armies of heaven followed him. They worshipped the Lord of Lords and King of Kings.

Read Revelation 19:1-16.

Reading Questions

Which groups praised God by proclaiming "Hallelujah!"?

List at least three things those groups identified as worthy of praise.

What did the bride wear?

What names was the man on the horse given?

What offensive, or attack, weapon did the man have?

Old Testament Links

From the beginning of time, God has been worthy of all praise and honor and glory. In these verses, that truth becomes vivid through the imagery of celebration, union, and triumph. Yet long before John's vision, the praise, the marriage of the Lamb, and the coming judgement were themes from of old – images seen dimly through glass. The images continue to be mysterious, but the sense of triumph resounds.

Read Hosea 2:16-20, Isaiah 61:10-11, and Ezekiel 16:8-13. How do these passages deepen understanding of the bride of the Lamb? What do you notice about the clothing and preparation for marriage?

Read Isaiah 62:1-5 and 63:1-3. How do these images reflect the vision recorded in Revelation 19:11-16? According to these passages, how does God feel about his people?

Application

Worship is often associated with music or singing in church, but at its core, it's about expressing how worthy God is – for who he is as well as what he has done. What reasons do you have for worshipping God? In what ways do you regularly worship him?

Because of Jesus, judgment is no longer something to fear as he has paid the price for what we have done. What matters now is the readiness and preparation for his return, a response to what he has already done. How can you stay spiritually ready and live in light of your salvation?

Session 14: The Book of Life

Revelation 19:17-20:15

Opening

Have you kept a journal or diary? What do you think of keeping a record of your life's events? What do you think of biographies or memoirs?

What kind of consequences feel right when someone breaks a rule – for example in a game, at work or in community? Has the punishment ever seemed too light or too harsh?

John's vision of war, victory, judgement, and a thousand-year reign flow quickly through this reading. With the beasts defeated, Satan bound, and the judgement delivered, the scenes remain mysterious. Though theologians continue to discuss the meaning of these events, the emphasis of God's authority and justice continues to capture the reader's attention.

Read Revelation 19:17–20:15.

Reading Questions

Who went to war with the armies of heaven?

What happened to the beasts and their followers?

What was the result of the dragon being sent into the abyss?

John's vision included the reign of Christ for 1,000 years. Who reigned with him?

What two things did Satan do when he was released from prison? What was his end?

What was recorded in the book of life? If a person's name was not in it, what happened to them?

Old Testament Links

Christ triumphs over his enemies not once but multiple times in Revelation 19:17-20:15. Though war is only one part of the account told through John's vision, much of it draws on images first introduced in the Old Testament – reminders of the Lord's might and judgement. Yet the backdrop to all of this is mercy: God offered invitation after invitation – calls to return, to repent, to receive - before this final reckoning.

Read Daniel 7:9-14 and Malachi 3:16-4:6. What parallels do you find between these passages and Revelation 19:17-20:15? Which portions may feel more mysterious now when read through the lens of multiple visions and prophecies instead of one?

Read Psalm 2:1-12. How does the Psalm deepen understanding of God's authority and final victory as portrayed in Revelation 19:17-20:15?

Application

What kinds of choices or accomplishments do you think leave a lasting legacy? Are there any values that you want to be more intentional about displaying in your daily life, knowing that you are seen, known, and loved?

Some things seem unfair, and we can struggle with why God allows certain evens to occur. Are there areas where you struggle to trust God's justice? What helps you release control or lean more fully into trusting him?

Session 15: A New Heaven and a New Earth

Revelation 21:1–22:21

Opening

For many, the new year offers a time to start over. We wipe the slate clean and begin again. What kinds of things do people tend to do start fresh in a new season?

Home is often where we feel most safe, known and cared for. What makes a place feel like home to you?

John's vision concludes with breathtaking hope. After the battles, judgement, and tribulation, the final chapters offer the promise of restoration – a new heaven, a new earth, and a home where God dwells with his people. The images are both familiar and mysterious: light without sun, healing without pain, a city that needs no temple. The scenes invite awe and offer comfort. God's plan, begun so long ago comes to completion – not through destruction, but in renewal.

Read Revelation 21:1-22:21.

Reading Questions

What did John see coming down out of heaven? What was it compared to?

What were God's promises from the throne?

What adjectives and names were given to God and Jesus in Revelation 21-22?

Who will inherit from God? Who will not?

Describe the new Jerusalem in general terms as John saw it.

How often will the gates be shut? Why this frequency?

How did John describe the river in the city?

When is Jesus coming? How many times did he say he was coming?

Old Testament Links

The prophets and history of God's people have long spoken of the newness of life that would come in due time. Hope was offered in times of despair and promises of God's presence were given to sustain and encourage his people throughout their history. Hints of a new heaven and a new earth are sprinkled throughout the Scriptures, reminding believers that God's story was always moving toward restoration.

Read Isaiah 65:17-25. How does this passage vary from the Revelation account of the new heaven and new earth?

Read Ezekiel 47:1-12. What role did water play in the passage compared to Revelation 22:1-5?

Application

What are small but meaningful ways you can live today in light of what is coming – the time when God's justice, presence, and peace with be fully known? How do the promises of Revelation 21 and 22 shape your priorities?

Revelation ends with the picture of God dwelling fully with his people – no distance or separation. Yet Jesus has already promised to abide with us. What helps you nurture that closeness with God now, even as you look forward to the fullness of life with him?

Conclusion

The revelation of Jesus given to John calls readers to see clearly both the destruction of sin and the beauty of God's faithfulness. The letters to the churches offer encouragement and correction, with a call to remain faithful despite pressure. The visions that follow are vivid and at times overwhelming, yet they are threaded with hope: calls to witness, repent, endure, worship. Warnings and promises, judgement and mercy, each pairing reveals God's character. And at the heart of it all is Jesus – present, victorious, and coming again soon to make all things new.

How has the book of Revelation shaped your understanding of God's justice and mercy?

What promise or image from Revelation gives you hope as you wait for Christ's return?

What did you learn about God from this study?

What did you learn about yourself from this study?

Do you believe that Jesus is the Messiah, the Son of God and have you received life in his name? If so, describe the qualities of that life.

If this is the first time that you have answered yes to the call of following Jesus, please reach out to a local church or the author to share of your choice and find support for your new life.

To continue your deep dive into "Seeing the Old Testament in the Epistles", pick up Colossians to continue your study. Find it at your nearest retailer by scanning the QR code today.

Colossians
Bible
Study:
Live
Transformed

Also By Sarah K. Howley

Seeing the Old Testament in the Epistles
Ephesians: Experience God's Power
James: Know God's Wisdom
1&2 Thessalonians: Prepare for Christ's Return
Hebrews: Elevate Jesus
Philippians: Pursue Christ's Joy
1&2 Peter: Grow in Grace
Revelation: Worship the Lamb
Colossians: Live Transformed

The Son Reveals the Father
I Am: An 8-Session Study of John
Heart: A 12-Session Study of Luke
Word: An 11-Session Study of Matthew
King: An 8-Session Study of Mark
Our Trustworthy God: How Much God loves You, Joyfully
Engages with You, and Trusts You

Women of the Old Testament Bible Studies
Hope: A Bible Study of Women in Jesus' Lineage

Faith (coming 2026)
Love (coming 2026)

Alive Again Bible Study on Forgiveness
Alive Again: Find Healing in in Forgiveness
Alive Again Bible Study: Find Healing in Forgiveness
Alive Again Forgiveness Prayer Journal

About the Author

Sarah K. Howley is an author, speaker, and trained Christian counselor with over a dozen published Bible studies. She is the founder of InspiritEncourage, where she equips believers to engage Scripture with depth and joy. Sarah's studies are known for their biblical richness, relatable tone, and focus on helping readers find joy in the Lord. She and her husband invest in global initiatives for literacy and hunger relief.

You can find Sarah on Facebook and Instagram @inspiritencourage. To book Sarah as a speaker at your next event, please contact her through her website. For weekly encouragement and information on her latest releases, sign up for Sarah's newsletter at InspiritEncourage.com.

InspiritEncourage

www.ingramcontent.com/pod-product-compliance
Lightning Source LLC
Chambersburg PA
CBHW071534120626
46550CB00006B/2450